PRAYER

PARTICIPANT'S GUIDE

By Philip Yancey

The Jesus I Never Knew

What's So Amazing about Grace?

The Bible Jesus Read

Reaching for the Invisible God

Where Is God When It Hurts?

Disappointment with God

The Student Bible, General Edition (with Tim Stafford)

Meet the Bible (with Brenda Quinn)

Church: Why Bother?

Finding God in Unexpected Places

I Was Just Wondering

Soul Survivor

Rumors of Another World

Prayer: Does It Make Any Difference?

By Philip Yancey and Dr. Paul Brand

Fearfully and Wonderfully Made

In His Image

The Gift of Pain

In the Likeness of God

PHILIP YANCEY

PRAYER

Does It Make Any Difference?

SIX SESSIONS ON OUR RELATIONSHIP WITH GOD

PARTICIPANT'S GUIDE

Written by Stephen and Amanda Sorenson

ZONDERVAN®

ZONDERVAN.com/
AUTHORTRACKER
follow your favorite authors

Prayer Participant's Guide
Copyright © 2007 by Philip Yancey

Requests for information should be addressed to:

Zondervan, *Grand Rapids, Michigan* 49530

ISBN-10: 0-310-27527-X
ISBN-13: 978-0-310-27527-5

Interior design by Beth Shagene

Printed in the United States of America

09 10 11 12 13 • 23 22 21 20 19 18 17 16 15 14 13 12 11 10

CONTENTS

THE VIEW FROM ABOVE

—⚬⚬⚬—

LORD, our Lord, how majestic is your name in all the earth!
You have set your glory above the heavens....
When I consider your heavens, the work of your fingers,
the moon and the stars, which you have set in place,
what are mere mortals that you are mindful of them,
human beings that you care for them?
PSALM 8:1, 3–4

INTRODUCTION (6 MINUTES)

DVD Introduction by Philip Yancey

Questions to Think About

• How would you describe your experiences with prayer?

• What do you understand the purpose of prayer to be?

• What do you long to experience in your prayer life?

GROUP DISCOVERY (35 MINUTES)

DVD Teaching Notes

Lessons from the mountains

Catching a glimpse of the "God's Eye View"

Prayer: realigning our perspectives

We are not in control

God is not our accomplice

DVD Discussion

Prayer is the act of seeing reality from God's point of view.... In prayer I shift my point of view away from ... the speck that is myself. I gaze at the stars and recall what role I or any of us play in a universe beyond comprehension.

Prayer, p. 29

1. What is the God's Eye View that Philip describes? (MEMORY JOGGER: How did the hikers appear to Philip and his wife as they looked down from the summit ridge? What big impact did the lightning storm have on Philip's perception of life? When it comes to God's work, who is the "accomplice"?)

2. The video segment provided several examples of how our human perceptions of what is most important and how life ought to work stand in opposition to the God's Eye View of what is most important and how life really works.

   • In what ways do the messages of the world's view of life contrast with Jesus' message about what really matters in life?

   • What are some ways we might, as Philip suggests, correct the world's messages with the God's Eye View?

3. When we come face to face with the reality of how little control we have over our future, many of us get a little nervous. What do you think could happen in our prayer life and in our relationship with God if, in the midst of our uncertain future, we intentionally chose to "be still and know that [he is] God"?

Bible Exploration
Be Still and Know That I Am God

Every day my vision clouds over so that I perceive nothing but a world of matter. It requires a daily act of will to remember what Paul told the sophisticated crowd in Athens: "[God] is not far from each one of us. 'For in him we live and move and have our being'" (Acts 17:27–28).

Prayer, p. 22

1. We tend to rely on our own sufficiency, but the Bible repeatedly exposes the true nature of earthly life. What unmistakable message about the God's Eye View of life is communicated through Psalms 39:4; 90:12; James 4:13–14; and 1 Peter 1:24?

2. Job's trials challenged his perspective and led him to reflect intensely on his human condition and God's role in the world.

   • What did the Lord of the universe remind Job about when he was wallowing in self-pity and demanding that God respond to his theological queries? (See Job 38:4–11, and note that God's response continues through Job 40:2.)

   • In his great discourse, God didn't provide even one specific answer to Job's probing questions. But what did Job say in response to God's thundering query, "Who is this that obscures my plans with words without knowledge?" (Job 38:2), that shows he got God's message loud and clear? (See Job 42:1–6.)

3. Philip encourages us to recognize the importance of God's command in Psalm 46:10: "Be still, and know that I am God." He helps us realize that we are not in control of the world (or our futures) and that the appropriate response to our condition is to be still before our powerful and merciful God and turn over our concerns and problems to that God. Let's deepen our understanding of what God means by this command and explore how we might go about obeying it.

- Consider what the command means. The Latin imperative for "be still" is *vacate* (from which we get the word *vacation*), so God is inviting us to take a break and allow him to be God in our daily lives. In addition, the word translated "know" refers not only to intellectual knowledge but also to knowing God through worship and obedience. In your daily life, what might it look like to actually put into practice these definitions of stillness and knowledge?

- If we are honest, many of us don't find it easy to be still and "wait on God." We keep taking on responsibilities and trying to accomplish more and more in our own strength. Yet many faithful followers of God who have gone before us learned to live life with a keen awareness of God's perspective and our human frailty. What do you learn about "waiting on God" from the following testimonies of those who have gone before us?

The psalmist: "Take delight in the LORD and he will give you the desires of your heart. Commit your way to the LORD; trust in him and he will do this: He will make your righteous reward shine like the dawn, your vindication like the noonday sun. Be still before the LORD and wait patiently for him." (Psalm 37:4–7)

The apostle Peter: "Humble yourselves, therefore, under God's mighty hand, that he may lift you up in due time. Cast all your anxiety on him because he cares for you." (1 Peter 5:6–7)

Jesus: "So do not worry, saying, 'What shall we eat?' or 'What shall we drink?' or 'What shall we wear?' For the pagans run after all these things, and your heavenly Father knows that you need them. But seek first his kingdom and his righteousness, and all these things will be given to you as well." (Matthew 6:31–33)

The prophet Isaiah: "Yet the LORD longs to be gracious to you; therefore he will rise up to show you compassion. For the LORD is a God of justice. Blessed are all who wait for him!" (Isaiah 30:18)

Closing Group Discovery Discussion

Not all of us make a practice of climbing mountains that envelop us in reminders of the God's Eye View. Nevertheless, images of daily life can alert us to the God's Eye View that we otherwise might dismiss. A car racing through an intersection against the light can remind us, in much the same way a lightning bolt can, how much we don't control in our lives. A mass of commuters crowded onto a subway platform during rush hour can remind us, in much the same way a mountaintop view of distant hikers can, how small we really are. Which images in your daily world remind you of God's command: "Be still, and know that I am God" (Psalm 46:10)?

WRAP-UP (14 MINUTES)

DVD Wrap-up by Philip Yancey

Personal Reflection

It occurs to me, thinking about prayer, that most of the time I get the direction wrong. I start downstream with my own concerns and bring them to God. I inform God, as if God did not already know. I plead with God, as if hoping to change God's mind and overcome divine reluctance. Instead, I should start upstream where the flow begins.

When I shift direction, I realize that God already cares about my concerns — my uncle's cancer, world peace, a broken family, a rebellious teenager — more than I do. Grace, like water, descends to the lowest part. Streams of mercy flow. I begin with God, who bears primary responsibility for what happens on earth.

Prayer, p. 23

Using the image of trickling drops of water that collect and begin flowing in an ever-widening stream down the mountains, Philip encourages us to reflect on the God's Eye View and use it as a starting point for prayer. During this time of quiet, pray silently, using the following outline as a guide. This exercise will help prepare you to pray together as a group at the close of this session.

Start at the top, the high snowfield where God is.

- Reflect on who you are as a person of eternal destiny created in God's image. Make necessary corrections and confession to renew an open relationship with God.
- Meditate on who God is. Thank and praise God for being the loving, faithful Creator who continues to care for the vast, created universe. Thank and praise God for what has been given to you.

Shift your image of God's love and blessing to the trickles of water that join together and begin to form small pools and alpine ponds.

- Realizing that God already cares about the people you know and love, pray for those closest to you — your relatives, neighbors, friends — and picture God's grace and blessing flowing down into their lives.

Imagine the flow of God's love and blessings growing wider and deeper, overflowing the pond and racing down the mountainside in a gurgling stream.

- Pray for distant relatives, people in need, and national concerns and issues that are important to you such as homelessness, genocide, children of AIDS, impoverished people in your community, and so on.

Turn your gaze to the image of a vast reservoir of water.

- Imagine the whole scope of God's involvement in the world and pray about the work God is doing everywhere. Join with others to extend the widening circle of God's love to those who have not yet experienced it. Pray about your place in accomplishing God's work and, as Jesus commanded in Matthew 5:44, pray for your enemies — those who persecute you or make your life difficult.

Group Prayer

When doubts creep in and I wonder whether prayer is a sanctified form of talking to myself, I remind myself that the Son of God, who had spoken worlds into being and sustains all that exists, felt a compelling need to pray. He prayed as if it made a difference, as if the time he devoted to prayer mattered every bit as much as the time he devoted to caring for people.

Prayer, p. 79

Begin by praying aloud verses 8–13 of Psalm 145:

The LORD is gracious and compassionate, slow to anger and rich in love. The LORD is good to all; he has compassion on all he has made. All your works praise you, LORD; your faithful people extol you. They tell of the glory of your kingdom and speak of your might, so that all people may know of your mighty acts and the glorious splendor of your kingdom. Your kingdom is an everlasting kingdom, and your dominion endures through all generations. The LORD is trustworthy in all he promises and faithful in all he does.

Using the same images you used during your personal reflection time, continue to pray about your concerns and God's work in the world. Focus on:

- The trickles of your personal concerns
- God's grace and blessing flowing into the lives of those close to you
- The widening stream of needs in the world that are close to the heart of God
- The vast reservoir of God's divine work in the universe

PERSONAL JOURNEY:
TO DO ON YOUR OWN

Prayer has become for me much more than a shopping list of requests to present to God. It has become a realignment of everything. I pray to restore the truth of the universe, to gain a glimpse of the world, and of me, through the eyes of God. In prayer I shift my point of view away from my own natural selfishness. I climb above timberline and look down at the speck that is myself. I gaze at the stars and recall what role I or any of us play in a universe beyond comprehension. Prayer is the act of seeing reality from God's point of view.

Prayer, p. 29

Bible Discovery

As Philip shared in this session, prayer helps him regain sight of God's perspective on things; it restores his vision of life to one that more resembles God's. God longs to do the same for each of us. So take some time out from the busy demands of your life and accept God's invitation to be still, to be reminded of who God is, and to respond in light of God's perspective on the universe.

Read the following verses and meditate on what they say about God and how that relates to your concerns and priorities. Feel free to jot down some notes to help you remember how to focus on the God's Eye View whenever you approach God in prayer.

God as Creator
Nehemiah 9:6

Amos 4:13

The faithful and compassionate heart of God

Psalm 33:5

Psalm 106:1

Psalm 116:5

God's personal concern for individual people

2 Chronicles 16:9a

Psalm 33:13–15

Isaiah 40:28–29

John 3:16

God's awareness of our personal needs
Psalm 146:7

Matthew 6:25 – 26

God's commitment to act on our behalf and for our benefit
Deuteronomy 3:24

Isaiah 48:17

Our response to God
Jeremiah 9:24

SUPPLEMENTAL BIBLE DISCOVERY:
Praying for the Bigger Picture

Often the scope of our prayers is limited to what we want God to do for us. Yet God sees and acts in a realm far beyond our sight. Consider the following passages about personal prayers offered to God that in some way (perhaps unknown to the one who was praying) connected to the bigger picture of what God was doing. How did God respond? In what ways do these examples influence your desire to keep company with God through prayer?

1 Kings 18:22-24, 33-39

2 Kings 20:1-7; 2 Chronicles 32:27-31

Nehemiah 1:5-11; 2:4-8

Daniel 9:4-5, 17-19; 10:1-13

2 Corinthians 12:7-9

MY PRAYER JOURNAL

Prayer invites us to rest in the fact that God is in control, and the world's problems are ultimately God's, not ours. If I spend enough time with God, I will inevitably begin to look at the world with a point of view that more resembles God's own.

Prayer, p. 210

It's not easy to acknowledge God and, in Philip's words, "restore the truth of the universe." Each of us faces many distractions and the ongoing temptation to try to be like God rather than being still, getting to know God better, and trusting God to be God. Yet the practice of being still before God is the best way to renew our perspective on life.

Use the following pages to write down your thoughts and observations about prayer as well as the people, situations, concerns, aspirations, and needs for which you want to pray. Keep the God's Eye View in mind and give some thought as to where your prayer concerns fit within that broader perspective.

_____

_____

_____

_____

_____

_____

_____

_____

_____

_____

_____

Blessed are those who make the LORD their trust.

PSALM 40:4

Blessed are those who have learned to acclaim you,
who walk in the light of your presence, LORD.
PSALM 89:15

Prayer helps correct myopia, calling to mind a perspective I daily forget. I keep reversing roles, thinking of ways in which God should serve me, rather than vice versa.... Prayer raises my sight beyond the petty ... circumstances of daily life to afford a glimpse of that lofty perspective. I realize my tininess and God's vastness, and the true relation of the two. In God's presence, I feel small because I am small.

Prayer, pp. 21 – 22

WHY PRAY?

—⚬⚬⚬—

Very early in the morning, while it was still dark,
Jesus got up, left the house and went off to a solitary place,
where he prayed.
MARK 1:35

INTRODUCTION (5 MINUTES)

DVD Introduction by Philip Yancey

Questions to Think About

- When we consider just how small we are in comparison to the vast expanse of the universe, what makes it possible for us to believe that prayer is worthwhile?

- How can we know that our prayers actually make a difference?

GROUP DISCOVERY (38 MINUTES)

DVD Teaching Notes

Jesus, the "magnifying glass" of faith

Questions about prayer

- Is it worthwhile?

- Does it make a difference?

- Why pray about what God already knows?

- Does God really care?

Lessons from the prayers of Jesus

DVD Discussion

Jesus knew how the universe worked. He had lived in heaven and he lived on earth. He knew that prayer was a way to bring God and us human beings together. So, whenever something important happened in Jesus' life, you'd find him at prayer.

From the video

1. When Philip faces difficult questions about God, faith, and prayer, why does he look to the teachings and earthly life of Jesus for answers?

2. What do you think is the real point of talking to God about the needs and concerns of your life?

3. How would you describe the relationship between prayer, God's will being done in heaven, and our ability to do God's will on earth?

Bible Exploration
The Prayer Life of Jesus under the Magnifying Glass

Jesus valued prayer enough to spend many hours at the task. If I had to answer the question "Why pray?" in one sentence, it would be, "Because Jesus did." He bridged the vast gulf between God and human beings. While on earth he became vulnerable, as we are vulnerable; rejected, as we are rejected; and tested, as we are tested. In every case his response was prayer.

Prayer, p. 50

1. Jesus, the Son of God, knows better than anyone how the universe works. After all, before he came to earth, he spoke worlds into being and sustained all that exists. Yet while Jesus was on earth, the Gospels tell us that he frequently prayed. In each of the following situations, why do you think prayer was important to Jesus? What you think Jesus wanted to accomplish by his prayers?

Matthew 14:8–15, 19–23

Mark 1:29–37

Luke 6:12–13

Luke 22:39–46

2. Jesus not only prayed when he faced the daunting challenges and opportunities of life, he also prayed as he went about the daily business of accomplishing God's work on earth. As you read each of the following passages, notice what Jesus prayed for. Focus your attention on what Jesus' example teaches us about prayer and the ways, if any, that his prayers differ from our normal pattern.

Bible Passage	What Jesus Prayed For	What His Example Teaches	How His Prayers Differ from Ours
Matt. 19:13–15			
Mark 6:41–44			
Luke 22:31–32			
Luke 23:33–34			
John 11:38–42			
John 14:16–18			
John 17:20–23			

Closing Group Discovery Discussion

In prayer we stand before God to plead our condition as well as the conditions around us. In the process, the act of prayer emboldens me to join the work of transforming the world into a place where the Father's will is indeed done as it is in heaven. We are Christ's body on earth, after all; he has no hands but ours. And yet to act as Christ's body we need an unbroken connection to the Head. We pray in order to see the world with God's eyes, and then to join the stream of power as it breaks loose.

Prayer, p. 124

For Jesus, prayer was the lifeline that connected him with his Father and his Father's will. We've seen several examples that show how important prayer was to Jesus. John 17:6–19 records a prayer that Jesus offered on behalf of his disciples shortly before his departure from earth. What in his prayer indicates that prayer would also be essential in the lives of his disciples (then and now) as they continued God's work on earth?

Jesus didn't stop praying for his disciples after he ascended to heaven. In fact, the New Testament's only glimpse of what Jesus is doing right now depicts him at the right hand of God where "he always lives to intercede" for us (Hebrews 7:25). Just as Jesus once prayed for Peter and his disciples, he now prays for us. What does it mean to you that Jesus makes prayer one of his primary tasks? What does his example of ongoing prayer for us reveal about the importance of prayer? If Jesus continues to participate in God's work through prayer, how significant is it that we too can participate in God's work through prayer?

WRAP-UP (12 MINUTES)

DVD Wrap-up by Philip Yancey

Jesus clung to prayer as to a lifeline, for it gave him both the guidance and the energy to know and do the Father's will. To maintain belief in the "real" world from which he came, to nourish memory of eternal light, he had to work at it all night on occasion, or rise before daybreak.

Prayer, p. 80

Personal Reflection

It's no secret that evil is at work in our world. We live on a planet ruled by powers intent on blocking and perverting the will of God, but God calls us to ally with his forces on earth to battle evil. Just as prayer was Jesus' lifeline in accomplishing God's work on earth, prayer is our lifeline. It is the means by which God invites us to bring the stuff of our world—the rhythms of nature, harassing problems, disturbed emotions, personality conflicts—and request a new perspective and new energy to accomplish God's work in our imperfect world.

Prayer reminds us of the truth of the universe: that no matter how challenging and difficult life is or how out of control the world seems, the God of mercy, justice, and fairness is in control. Take the next few minutes to reflect on what you have discovered so far about how Jesus prayed. As you read the following Bible passages, focus your attention on how they apply to your life and relationship with God. Consider how you can direct your prayers to reconnect with God who is accomplishing his great purpose in the universe.

Pray because it matters.

> Finally, be strong in the Lord and in his mighty power. Put on the full armor of God, so that you can take your stand against the devil's schemes. For our struggle is not against flesh and blood, but against the rulers, against the authorities, against the powers of this dark world and against the spiritual forces of evil in the heavenly realms. (Ephesians 6:10–12)

> The weapons we fight with are not the weapons of the world. On the contrary, they have divine power to demolish strongholds. (2 Corinthians 10:4)

> "Watch and pray so that you will not fall into temptation." (Mark 14:38)

Pray with confidence that God desires to respond.

> "Your Father knows what you need before you ask him." (Matthew 6:8)

> Let us then approach God's throne of grace with confidence, so that we may receive mercy and find grace to help us in our time of need. (Hebrews 4:16)

As a father has compassion on his children, so the LORD has compassion on those who fear him. (Psalm 103:13)

Pray for the will of heaven.

"This, then, is how you should pray: 'Our Father in heaven, hallowed be your name, your kingdom come, your will be done, on earth as it is in heaven. Give us today our daily bread.'" (Matthew 6:9–11)

Ask for the help of heaven.

And pray that we may be delivered from wicked and evil people, for ... the Lord is faithful, and he will strengthen you and protect you from the evil one. (2 Thessalonians 3:2–3)

"If you remain in me and my words remain in you, ask whatever you wish, and it will be done for you." (John 15:7)

Is anyone among you in trouble? Let them pray. (James 5:13)

Truly my soul finds rest in God; my salvation comes from him. Truly he is my rock and my salvation; he is my fortress, I will never be shaken. (Psalm 62:1–2)

Group Prayer

Take a few minutes to pray about your concerns and God's work in the world. Begin by praying aloud Psalm 34:4–8:

I sought the LORD, and he answered me; he delivered me from all my fears. Those who look to him are radiant; their faces are never covered with shame. This poor man called, and the LORD heard him; he saved him out of all his troubles. The angel of the LORD encamps around those who fear him, and he delivers them. Taste and see that the LORD is good; blessed are those who take refuge in him.

Remember, we have no more powerful way to bring together the visible and invisible worlds than through prayer. Prayer allows us to recharge our batteries. It allows us to present our world, whatever its circumstances, to God and ask for divine help in equipping us to counter the forces of evil. Take this opportunity as you pray to reconnect, refocus, and realign your hearts with God's unfolding plan for the world.

PERSONAL JOURNEY:
TO DO ON YOUR OWN

God desires an ongoing relationship with us, and prayer closes the vast gap between infinity and us. It's a way of keeping company with God, who is already present, and responding to his presence. Prayer is where God and human beings meet, a way of asking God to pour some eternity into us.

From the video

Bible Discovery

Paul wrote to the Ephesians, "For we are God's handiwork, created in Christ Jesus to do good works" (2:10). *Handiwork* conveys rather clumsily the meaning of the Greek word *poiema*, from which we get the English word *poem*. So Paul is saying that we are God's work of art. With his history of beatings, prison, shipwreck, and riots, who better than Paul knew the travail involved in the fashioning of that art—and the role that prayer played. Prayer offers an opportunity for God to remodel us, to chisel marble like a sculptor, touch up colors like an artist, edit words like a writer.

Prayer accomplishes its work because it connects our heart with the heart of God. As Philip states in the video, "God doesn't need the 'data' of my life. What he cares about is my heart. He wants me to spend time with him so that I can share my passions, my concern, what I really care about."

In the Hebrew context, heart (*lev*) is the core of a person's being, the inner person, the center from which all else flows. It is the seat of affection and source of action. So let's explore what God says about heart and why a heart that loves, seeks, and desires to obey God is such a treasure.

1. To what extent does God know our heart—our deepest desires, the core of our being?

   • 1 Chronicles 29:17–18

• Psalm 44:20–21

• Jeremiah 17:10

• Luke 16:15

2. The passages below and on page 34 reveal various ways we can demonstrate our heart commitment to God. Prayerfully consider how each one can strengthen the connection between your heart and God's, then make a conscious effort to do them as you go about your daily life.

Bible Passage	How to Demonstrate a Heart Commitment to God	How to Demonstrate My Heart Commitment in My Daily Life
1 Sam. 12:24		
Ps. 9:1–2		
Ps. 62:7–8		
Ps. 112:7		
Ps. 119:9–10		

Bible Passage	How to Demonstrate a Heart Commitment to God	How to Demonstrate My Heart Commitment in My Daily Life
Ps. 119:57–58		
Ps. 119:69–71		
Prov. 3:5–6		
Matt. 22:37		
Rom. 1:9		

SUPPLEMENTAL BIBLE DISCOVERY:
What Kind of Heart Does God Treasure?

The Bible has much to say about the hearts of those who seek after God. Yet how much do we know about a heart that longs to keep company with God? Take a look at the following passages to discover some of the qualities of such a heart.

- 2 Kings 22:19

- Psalm 51:10

- Psalm 57:7

- Psalm 86:11

- Psalm 125:4

- Hebrews 10:22

MY PRAYER JOURNAL

I pray in astonished belief that God desires an ongoing relationship. I pray in trust that the act of prayer is God's designated way of closing the vast gulf between infinity and me. I pray in order to put myself in the stream of God's healing work on earth. I pray as I breathe—because I can't help it.

Prayer, p. 326

During session two, you explored Jesus' commitment to prayer, God's promises concerning your prayers, and the power of prayer in combating evil. Feel free to use the following pages to write down some things you learned about prayer, God, and yourself; prayer requests; people for whom you plan to pray; and any sins that have created distance between you and God.

Remember, prayer is the means by which we bring who we really are—our honest selves—to God and gain the resources and strength to go out and do the Father's will on earth. Prayer invites God into your world and ushers you into God's. Just as Jesus counted on prayer as a source of strength to equip him to carry out a partnership with God the Father on earth, you can admit your dependence on God and receive the blessings promised in return.

Come near to God and he will come near to you.
Wash your hands, you sinners, and purify your hearts,
you double-minded.
JAMES 4:8

Let the hearts of those who seek the LORD rejoice.
1 CHRONICLES 16:10

_____

_____

_____

_____

_____

_____

_____

_____

_____

_____

_____

_____

_____

_____

_____

_____

_____

_____

_____

Prayer remains a struggle for me.... I persist because I am fulfilling God's command, and also because I believe I am doing what is best for me whether or not I feel like it at the time. Moreover, I believe that my perseverance, in some unfathomable way, brings pleasure to God. We should always pray and not give up, Jesus taught.

Prayer, p. 161

KEEPING COMPANY
WITH GOD

The LORD is righteous in all his ways and faithful in all he does.
The LORD is near to all who call on him, to all who call on him in truth.
PSALM 145:17–18

INTRODUCTION (6 MINUTES)

DVD Introduction by Philip Yancey

Questions to Think About

- In what ways may our image of God affect our ability to come before God and reveal who we really are?

- Which wrong images of God might we need to "fire" in order to get to know God better?

GROUP DISCOVERY (36 MINUTES)

DVD Teaching Notes

A different view of prayer

- Making yourself known to God

- Learning who God is

Images of getting close to God

Engaging with the God of the universe

DVD Discussion

I realize that my image of God, more than anything else, determines my degree of honesty in prayer. . . . Foolishly, I hide myself in fear that God will be displeased, though in fact the hiding may be what displeases God most. From my side, the wall seems like self-protection; from God's side it looks like lack of trust. In either case, the wall will keep us apart until I acknowledge my need and God's surpassing desire to meet it.

Prayer, p. 44

---

1. Do you ever wish you could just spin a prayer wheel and receive all the benefits of prayer? If we're honest, most of us have to admit at least a little tendency to view prayer as an obligatory ritual or a necessary transaction between ourselves and God. What would you anticipate would change if we could shove aside our "prayer baggage" and welcome prayer as a privileged opportunity to share honestly who we really are with a loving, personal God?

2. To what extent do you think our view of God shapes our willingness to trust God?

3. How should the fact that God already knows the truth about each of us (and loves us anyway) influence our prayers and our willingness to trust God?

4. Philip talks about the importance of "keeping company with God."

- What practical, everyday things can we do that will help us tune in to God's presence and be honest with God about who we are?

- What part do you think confession of our faults and expression of our needs play in keeping company with God?

Bible Exploration
Engaging Honestly with God

We do not pray to tell God what he does not know, nor to remind him of things he has forgotten. He already cares for the things we pray about.... He has simply been waiting for us to care about them with him. When we pray, we stand by God and look with him toward those people and problems. When we lift our eyes from them toward him, we do so with loving praise, just as we look toward our oldest and dearest friends and tell them how we care for them, though they already know it.... We speak to him as we speak to our most intimate friends — so that we can commune together in love.

Tim Stafford, quoted in *Prayer*, p. 58

1. It is hard to have a close relationship with someone when we keep our feelings and thoughts to ourselves. Yet that is what many of us try to do in our prayer relationship with God. Perhaps we do it because we are aware of our failures, weaknesses, and needs and don't want to be vulnerable or "look bad" before God. But the amazing thing is, God still loves us, more than we can imagine, and longs to share an intimate relationship with each of us.

   • How much about us — what we think, feel, do, say — does God already know? (See Psalm 139:1 – 4, 23 – 24.)

   • Is there any way for us to hide the truth about ourselves from God? Why or why not? (See Psalm 33:13 – 15.)

• Philip writes that one way he knows about God's compassionate love is "because of Jesus: I see the tears of compassion he wept for Mary and Martha; I see the physical healing Jesus provided every time he was asked; I see the transformations he worked in prostitutes and tax collectors and social outcasts. I gain peace when I realize that I do not have to talk God into caring. God cares more than I can imagine, and has ultimate control over all that happens" (*Prayer*, p. 272). Can you think of other Bible passages that speak of God's unquenchable love for you?

2. Opening ourselves up and being honest with God about who we really are essential components of keeping company with God through all of life. In fact, such honesty gives God pleasure!

   • In what ways does asking God to show us our sins and then confessing them to him help us make ourselves known to God and restore our relationship? (See Psalms 32:1–2; 51:10–12.)

   • What part does confession play in gaining perspective on our proper place in God's world? (See 2 Chronicles 7:14.)

3. Some of us think we must "put on a good show" for God. When we approach him we may tend to gloss over our nagging spiritual questions, try to hide our sin, and pretend that our pain doesn't hurt as bad as it does. But Philip sees prayer as an opportunity to bring our doubts,

complaints, failures, and sins before God and engage that part of our life with God. In fact, Philip takes the opportunity of prayer so seriously that he says, "If I march through life pretending to smile when inside I bleed, in a pitiful attempt to handle life without God, I dishonor the relationship." What can we learn about engaging with God and sharing what's *really* inside us from the following honest expressions of the heart? In what ways, if any, do these prayers differ from your own?

• Psalm 3:7

• Psalm 13:1 – 3

• Psalm 22:1 – 2

• Psalm 144:6

• Jeremiah 12:1

• Habakkuk 1:2 – 3

Closing Group Discovery Discussion

First Peter 5:5 – 7 reveals humility as a necessary heart attitude in approaching God: "'God opposes the proud but shows favor to the humble and oppressed.' Humble yourselves, therefore, under God's mighty hand, that he may lift you up in due time. Cast all your anxiety on him because he cares for you." It seems, then, that humility enables us to gain a glimpse of our true state in the universe—our smallness in light of God's greatness. Humility makes it possible for us to admit our need so that God can lift us up.

Yet we live in a culture that emphasizes personal strength and self-reliance. That creates some problems. As Philip observes, "In a paradox that I keep forgetting, God needs my confessed weakness far more than my strength. By trying to be strong, I may even block God's power." Take a few minutes to discuss the challenges we must overcome in order to humble ourselves before God and keep company with him.

WRAP-UP (13 MINUTES)

DVD Wrap-up by Philip Yancey

Personal Reflection

Unless I level with God—about bitterness over an unanswered prayer, grief over loss, guilt over an unforgiving spirit, a baffling sense of God's absence ... I may continue going to church, singing hymns and praise choruses, even addressing God politely in formal prayers, but I will never break through the intimacy barrier.

Prayer, p. 42

Prayer, especially honest prayer, brings us and God together; it allows our true selves to be loved by God. But many do not view prayer as the "safe place" where we open up, let down our masks, and expose our real selves to God. The challenge is to bring together who God really is and who we really are. Because of our flawed images of God and our tendency to avoid vulnerability with God, most of us will need to work on both of these areas.

Take a couple of minutes to reflect on the following passages. Consider what they mean in light of your unique circumstances and your personal prayer journey with God.

Pray continually, give thanks in all circumstances; for this is God's will for you in Christ Jesus. (1 Thessalonians 5:17–18)

The LORD is a refuge for the oppressed, a stronghold in times of trouble. Those who know your name trust in you, for you, LORD, have never forsaken those who seek you. (Psalm 9:9–10)

To keep me from becoming conceited, I was given a thorn in my flesh, a messenger of Satan, to torment me. Three times I pleaded with the Lord to take it away from me. But he said to me, "My grace is sufficient for you, for my power is made perfect in weakness." (2 Corinthians 12:7–9)

If we confess our sins, [God] is faithful and just and will forgive us our sins and purify us from all unrighteousness. (1 John 1:9)

Let us then approach God's throne of grace with confidence, so that we may receive mercy and find grace to help us in our time of need. (Hebrews 4:16)

"Call to me and I will answer you and tell you great and unsearchable things you do not know." (Jeremiah 33:3)

Now consider what you will do to open up a more authentic and honest relationship with God through prayer:

- Which preconceptions of God are hindering an intimate prayer relationship with God? (Be honest!)

- Begin making a list of your fears, anxieties, secrets—the kinds of things that you don't easily tell people—to share with God.

If you are willing, let God know you are ready to step out in faith and make yourself vulnerable. God longs for you to share with him what the Japanese call your *honne*—the inner self you carefully protect from most people. The very weaknesses that drive us to pray invite God to respond with compassion and power.

Group Prayer

"We cannot make [God] visible to us, but we can make ourselves visible to Him," said Abraham Joshua Heschel. I make the attempt with hesitation, shame, and fear, but when I do so I often find those constraints dissolving. My fear of rejection yields to God's embrace. Somehow, in a way I can only trust and not understand, presenting to God the intimate details of my life gives God pleasure.

Prayer, p. 43

Begin by praying aloud Psalm 103:10–14:

[God] does not treat us as our sins deserve or repay us according to our iniquities. For as high as the heavens are above the earth, so great is his love for those who fear him; as far as the east is from the west, so far has he removed our transgressions from us. As a father has compassion on his children, so the LORD has compassion on those who fear him; for he knows how we are formed, he remembers that we are dust.

Now continue to pray, focusing on our appropriate place of deep need before God so that God, in turn, can lift us up. Thank God for his love and commitment to handle anything we present. Ask God to help us discover more of who he is.

PERSONAL JOURNEY: TO DO ON YOUR OWN

Once, I took a sequence of ten psalms (35–44) and listed other principles of prayer I had learned from them. I found that the psalms broadened my notion of prayer by taking more risks, demanding more of the relationship, expressing more passion. In short, they exposed the shallowness of my own prayers and challenged me to engage with God at a deeper level.... I learned from Psalms to converse with God as I would converse with my employer, my friend, my wife—in short, to treat God as a Person in every sense of the word. I had seen prayer as a kind of duty, not as a safe outlet for whatever I was thinking or feeling. Psalms freed me to go deeper.

Prayer, pp. 175–176

Bible Discovery

The book of Psalms is a collection of 150 prayers. Philip calls it a "practicum in prayer." In this ready-made prayer book, we find prayers that fit any mood and encompass all human experience. These prayers bare the human soul before God in a way that strikes a universal chord and they also offer deep insights into the safe outlet God desires prayer to be for us. Using the Psalms as your guide, take some time to explore how appropriate it is to voice fear, anger, insecurity, doubt, thankfulness—or anything else we need to express—in our prayers to God.

1. Look up each of the following verses from Psalms and write out what they reveal about (1) the psalmists' prayer requests, and (2) what you can share honestly with God.

Psalm Portion	What the Psalmists Prayed About	What I Can Honestly Pray About
3:5–8		
13:1–3		
17:6–9		
22:1–2		
23:1–3		
25:4–7		
37:4		
40:17		
42:9		
51:1–4, 8–12		
57:1		

Psalm Portion	What the Psalmists Prayed About	What I Can Honestly Pray About
61:1 – 3		
74:10 – 11		
86:15 – 17		
88:1 – 5		
119:153 – 156		
138:8		
139:14		
142:5 – 6		
144:5 – 8		

2. Remember the list of fears, anxieties, and secrets that you began writing during your personal reflection time? Take time now to complete that list. As you continue your prayer journey with God, begin opening these deepest parts of your self. God can handle whatever you reveal. Give yourself the opportunity to get to know God as a Person of mercy, love, compassion, and understanding.

SUPPLEMENTAL BIBLE DISCOVERY:
Afraid to Wrestle with God?

God invites us to wrestle with him in prayer: to persistently present our honest selves; to cling to God in the dark without letting go; to call God to account for his promises and character. The following passages reveal dialogue between God and faithful people of the Bible who stood toe-to-toe and "wrestled" with God. Note what these historical encounters reveal about God, about honestly wrestling with God in prayer, and the kind of people God chooses to accomplish his work.

Abraham, who kept appealing to God's grace and mercy
Genesis 18:17 - 19, 22 - 33

Jacob, who literally wrestled all night with God
Genesis 32:22 - 28

Moses, who argued and negotiated with God
Exodus 3:1 - 17; 4:1 - 17; 32:1 - 14; Numbers 11:4 - 17, 21 - 25

Jesus, who wrestled with his Father concerning the trials he was facing
Matthew 26:36 - 42

Ananias, who questioned God's command
Acts 9:10 - 16

MY PRAYER JOURNAL

Psalms keeps me honest by furnishing words to prayers I would not pray apart from their prompting. I have learned to pray more *humanly* by reading the psalms and making them my prayers. As I read the psalms of anger and revenge, I have to face the same tendencies in myself. The psalms expose to the light resentments and wounds long buried. I find it liberating that God welcomes, even encourages, me to face into my dark side in my prayers. I can trust God with my secrets.

Prayer, pp. 173–174

If you want to keep company with God, it's essential that you make yourself known to God. God loves and cares for you and is big enough to handle your concerns, doubts, questions, anger, sorrow, and pain.

Use the following pages to write out prayer requests or thoughts about God and prayer. You may even find it helpful to rewrite psalms in your own words, substituting particulars of thanks, anguish, or petition for the original words. Feel free to journal about things that you have tried to hide from God and how you think God feels in response.

_____

_____

_____

_____

_____

_____

_____

_____

_____

As the deer pants for streams of water, so my soul pants for you, my God.
My soul thirsts for God, for the living God.
PSALM 42:1–2

Come near to God and he will come near to you....
Humble yourselves before the Lord, and he will lift you up.
JAMES 4:8, 10

"We must lay before Him what is in us, not what ought to be in us," wrote C. S. Lewis. To put it another way, we must trust God with what God already knows.

Prayer, p. 42

HOW TO PRAY

—⚭—

Give praise to the LORD, call on his name; . . .
let the hearts of those who seek the LORD rejoice.
Look to the LORD and his strength; seek his face always.
PSALM 105:1, 3 – 4

INTRODUCTION (5 MINUTES)

DVD Introduction by Philip Yancey

Questions to Think About

- Each of us has had unique experiences with prayer, and when we talk about those experiences honestly — revealing the negative as well as the positive — we often encourage one another to renew our efforts to keep company with God. Which word(s) would you use to describe the nature of your prayer practice? (Structured? Spontaneous? Erratic? Rushed? Meditative? Absent?)

- Which words best describe your level of satisfaction and fulfillment in your prayer life? (Confusing? Fulfilling? Frustrating?)

GROUP DISCOVERY (36 MINUTES)

DVD Teaching Notes

No prayer "formula"

Helpful hints

- Schedule specific times for prayer

- Ongoing conversations that help us "tune in" to God

- When nothing seems to work

DVD Discussion

Apart from the requirement that we be authentic before God, there is no prescribed way to pray. Each of us presents a unique mix of personality, outlook, training, gifts, and weaknesses, as well as a unique history with church and with God. As Roberta Bondi says, "If you are praying, you are already 'doing it right.'"

Prayer, p. 190

1. Philip has concluded that no formula for prayer works for everyone. He writes, "I must find my own way to pray, not someone else's. And as life changes, my prayer practice will no doubt change with it" (*Prayer,* p. 163).

   • What reasons does he offer for not depending on a prayer formula, and how does this perspective differ from other teaching you have heard or read? (MEMORY JOGGER: Think of personality differences, prayer styles, lifestyles, and desert times.)

   • In what ways might this perspective affect your efforts to pray?

2. Just because there is no one formula for prayer does not dismiss the need for a disciplined prayer life. What are some benefits of reserving a specific time for prayer each day to review what our recent days have encompassed, anticipate what the next days will bring, and commit each day to God—just as we would schedule time for physical exercise, eating, and watching the news?

3. The command to pray continually (1 Thessalonians 5:17) can be intimidating, but Philip presents several ways we can integrate prayer into everyday life. What specific things can we use as "reminders" to pray during our busy days, and how do these help us "tune in" to God's presence and plan as we go about our activities?

Bible Exploration
"Showing Up" for Prayer

For years I resisted a regular routine of prayer, believing that communication with God should be spontaneous and free. As a result I prayed infrequently and with little satisfaction. Eventually I learned that spontaneity often flows from discipline. Leonardo da Vinci spent ten years drawing ears, elbows, hands, and other parts of the body in many different aspects. Then one day he set aside the exercises and painted what he saw. Likewise, athletes and musicians never become great without regular practice. I found that I needed the discipline of regularity to make possible those exceptional times of free communication with God. . . . As with physical exercise, much of the benefit of prayer comes as a result of consistency, the simple act of showing up.

Prayer, p. 166

Philip has found that developing a meaningful prayer life has more to do with consistently "showing up" and actually praying than in finding a formula for prayer, reading more prayer books, listening to more prayer tapes, or attending prayer seminars. Even so, it is important for each of us to know why we pray and to find effective practices that help us pray—habits and reminders that fit our personalities, daily schedules, and prayer styles.

1. When Jesus lived on earth, prayer was as essential to him as food. His disciples recognized the uniqueness of his prayer life and sought to pray as he did. They prayed intently and also taught other believers to pray. Acts 10:1–2; Colossians 4:2; 1 Thessalonians 3:10; 5:17; and 1 Timothy 5:5 provide glimpses of prayer in the lives of early Christians. Read each passage and consider the following questions:

   • How serious were they about prayer, and what role did it play in their lives?

• What were some of their regular practices and purposes in prayer?

• In what way were their prayers "connected" with their daily life and God's work on earth?

2. How much freedom do we have in the way we pray? The Bible provides numerous images of the prayer habits and patterns of those who have gone before us. What do you learn from the following examples of prayer about keeping company with God? In what ways, if any, do they inspire you to pray?

Bible Passage	When (and Why) People Prayed	How I Would Like to Pray Differently
1 Sam. 15:10–11; Luke 6:12–13		
Ezra 9:3–6		
Ps. 5:3		
Dan. 6:6–10		
Acts 16:22–25		

3. Sometimes, despite our best efforts, prayer just doesn't seem to be working. We may even reach a point of discouragement or exhaustion where we cannot voice even a word to God in prayer. Yet it is important that we still "show up" in whatever state we find ourselves.

   • Regardless of apparent success or failure in relating to God through prayer, how can we be certain that even our wordlessness finds its way to the Source, that our interests will be communicated to God? (See Romans 8:26–27.)

   • What encouragement does this commitment on God's part provide? How should it affect our prayers through difficult times?

WRAP-UP (14 MINUTES)

DVD Wrap-up by Philip Yancey

Wrap-up Discussion

The common danger we face ... is getting so absorbed in daily life that we simply fail to show up. Any visitor to a Muslim country can see the difference. Five times a day, when the call to prayer goes out, all work and commerce stops, buses and trains empty, and faithful Muslims roll out a prayer rug, bowing low to say their prayers. Christians have no such ritual to stop and remember God. It's up to us.

Prayer, p. 182

What are some of the things that make prayer work for you? What type of setting do you find best for regular communication with God? What time of day works best for you and why? How beneficial to your communion with God is it to have inner conversations with God all day long?

Ideas you come up with may include:

- Setting aside at least one specific time each day for prayer
- Creating an environment for prayer — perhaps lighting a candle or playing music in the background while you pray
- Discovering a specific place that stimulates you to pray — an outdoor garden, a quiet corner in your local library, a particular chair in your home, sitting in your car during your lunch break
- Meditating on how God must feel about the issues and people for whom you pray
- Daily reviewing with God what happened in your life that day
- Identifying reminders that encourage you to pray continually

Personal Reflection

I have sampled various [prayer] methods from time to time and find them useful as long as I think of them as a supporting structure, a sort of scaffolding, rather than a rigid formula I must follow. The goal is to spend time with God, not to follow a legalistic procedure. If a system helps achieve that ultimate goal, fine. If not, I move on. Moods change, life goes through seasons, personalities differ. Each person who prays will need to find a rhythm or method that fits, for each of us has a unique privilege of offering love and attention to the One who made and sustains us.

Prayer, p. 181

Have you ever wondered why life conspires against having regular, satisfying prayer times? It's easy to get "too busy" to pray or to conclude that effective prayer is too complicated. It's easy to lose sight of who God really is and assume God can't possibly care about our prayers. Add in other hindrances such as the barrage of "noise" in our fast-paced, information- and entertainment-driven society, and prayer often gets overlooked or simply drowned out. Fortunately, we have the freedom to find our own ways to pray—ways that fit who we are, our circumstances, our needs and not those of someone else.

During the next few minutes:

- Think about who God is and why daily prayer is important to you (and to God).
- Begin planning how to create (or expand) space in your day for prayer.
- Ponder what you might do to remind yourself to pray continually and "tune in" to God's presence as you go through each day.
- Choose what you will try this week—something you've never tried before—to stimulate your prayer life.

Most important, commit yourself to faithfully "show up" and pray—not just think or talk about prayer. Ask for guidance and encouragement as you seek to keep company with God.

Group Prayer

Begin by praying aloud in the manner Jesus taught his disciples to pray (Matthew 6:9–13):

> "This, then, is how you should pray: 'Our Father in heaven, hallowed be your name, your kingdom come, your will be done on earth as it is in heaven. Give us today our daily bread. Forgive us our debts, as we also have forgiven our debtors. And lead us not into temptation, but deliver us from the evil one.'"

Now continue to pray, focusing on your desire and commitment to "show up" and keep company with God in the midst of life. Ask God to help you encourage one another in prayer. Ask for help to pray continually and to become more aware of the times your everyday life intersects with what is important to God.

PERSONAL JOURNEY: TO DO ON YOUR OWN

Besides teaching the "grammar" of prayer, studying the Bible affords a glimpse of the broad sweep of God's actions in history. It gets my own life off center stage. I learn the wisdom of reviewing the big picture, of placing my own small story in the context of God's story. I learn that I am not the only one who has wrestled with God or who has endured a time of wilderness and testing. I learn how to adore God, something that does not come naturally to me. Prayers based on the Bible help me recognize God's voice.

Prayer, p. 178

Bible Discovery

"Prayer," Philip reminds us, "is a way of relating to God, not a skill set like double-entry bookkeeping." So learning to pray takes time. It involves discovery, successes, and setbacks. The intimacy we long for in our prayer relationship with God will ebb and flow. Fortunately, people have been praying for a very long time, so we have many mentors to instruct, guide, and encourage us as we continue on our personal prayer journey.

1. The Bible includes approximately 650 prayers of faithful believers who have gone before us. These prayers show how people experiencing a variety of moods and circumstances have talked to God about important matters throughout history. They offer insight into prayer and how to pray. During the coming weeks, begin reading the prayers of the Bible. To get started, here and on the next page is a list of a few of the Bible's great prayers:

   • Genesis 18: Abraham's plea for Sodom
   • Exodus 15: Moses' song to the Lord
   • Exodus 33: Moses meets with God
   • 2 Samuel 7: David's response to God's promises
   • 1 Kings 8: Solomon's dedication of the temple
   • 2 Chronicles 20: Jehoshaphat prays for victory
   • Ezra 9: Ezra prays about the people's sins
   • Psalm 22: A cry to God for help

- Psalm 104: A prayer of praise
- Daniel 9: Daniel prays for forgiveness and Jerusalem's restoration
- Habakkuk 3: A prophet's prayer of acceptance
- Matthew 6: The Lord's prayer
- John 17: Jesus prays for himself, his disciples, and all believers
- Colossians 1: Paul's prayer of thanksgiving

2. In addition to studying the prayers of the Bible (and perhaps even memorizing them), we can gain helpful insights when we compare the prayers of different Bible characters. For example, read Ezra 9:6–15 and Nehemiah 1:5–2:5. Notice the differences between these prayers.

- Which approach to God is most like your own?

- What did each man pray for that was close to the heart of God? (Note how each man understood his place in the stream of what God was doing at the time.)

- In what ways do you think each man's relationship with God may have affected his everyday life, and how might these insights affect your everyday experience with God?

SUPPLEMENTAL BIBLE DISCOVERY:
Try This!

Paul's prayers, like the Psalms, give us a template for our own (see Ephesians 1:15 – 21; 3:14 – 21; Philippians 1:3 – 11; Colossians 1:9 – 12; 2 Thessalonians 1:11 – 12; Philemon 4 – 7). As you read them in his letters:

- *Ask:* What does Paul pray for? In what ways do his prayers reflect the truth that Jesus Christ is the center of the universe? For what is he thankful? About which practical matters does he pray?

- *Feel free* to use his prayers as a searchlight on yourself. Is your love abounding more and more in knowledge and depth as happened when Paul prayed for the Philippians?

- *Try inserting* the names of people you love into Paul's prayers. For example, if someone struggles with doubts, add his or her name into the sequence of Paul's prayer for the Ephesians.

MY PRAYER JOURNAL

Contact with God doesn't just provide a moment of spiritual ecstasy; it equips me for the rest of life. I corral a few minutes of calm in the morning in hopes that I can carry some part of that calm into the rest of the day. If I pray consistently I feel free and strong, able to meet the challenges and temptations of the day.

Prayer, p. 167

Keeping company with God is a very personal journey. Use the following pages to write out your prayer requests and prayer experiences. Write about your prayer "successes" as well as barriers to prayer such as false views of God, time/schedule issues, problems that seem too overwhelming to share with God.

As you pray, freely bring before God your thoughts and feelings. Invite God to teach you more about himself. Commit yourself to discovering the best ways not only to pray regularly but to become prayerfully aware of God's presence throughout your day. And no matter what, "show up." Your presence always gives God pleasure.

Let us then approach God's throne of grace with confidence,
so that we may receive mercy
and find grace to help us in our time of need.
HEBREWS 4:16

Blessed are those who have learned to acclaim you,
who walk in the light of your presence, Lord.
Psalm 89:15

Prayer is hardly a perfect form of communication, for I, an imperfect, material being who lives on an imperfect, material planet am reaching out for a perfect, spiritual Being. Some prayers go unanswered, a sense of God's presence ebbs and flows, and often I sense more mystery than resolution. Nevertheless I keep at it, believing with Paul that "now I know in part; then I shall know fully, even as I am fully known."

Prayer, pp. 326–327

PRAYER PROBLEMS

—⊸⊶⊷⊸—

Hear my cry, O God; listen to my prayer. From the ends of the earth
I call to you, I call as my heart grows faint; lead me to the rock that is higher
than I. For you have been my refuge, a strong tower against the foe. I long to
dwell in your tent forever and take refuge in the shelter of your wings.
PSALM 61:1–4

INTRODUCTION (5 MINUTES)

DVD Introduction by Philip Yancey

Questions to Think About

- On a scale from 1 to 10 (10 being the highest), how big a problem has unanswered prayer been in your relationship with God?

- How has unanswered prayer affected you and people you love?

- In what ways have unanswered prayers affected your relationship with and expectations of God?

GROUP DISCOVERY (40 MINUTES)

DVD Teaching Notes

Extravagant promises versus unanswered prayers

Why we may not get what we pray for

Telling God exactly what we want

Persistence matters

Trusting God for the "surprise factor"

DVD Discussion

Prayer does not work according to a fixed formula: get your life in order, say the right words, and the desired result will come. If that were true, Job would have avoided much suffering, Paul would have shed his thorn in the flesh, and Jesus would never have gone to Golgotha. Between the two questions "Does God answer prayer?" and "Will God grant my specific prayer for this sick child or this particular injustice?" lies a great pool of mystery.

Prayer, p. 230

---

1. There's no doubt that unanswered prayer can be very troubling and even discouraging. Although we may find no explanation as to why God doesn't answer a specific prayer, what have you seen happen — in terms of your relationship with God, your view of life, your self-examination, your commitment to action — when you must pray with persistence instead of making a request once and having God answer it as you would like?

2. Philip spoke of "editing" his prayers so that he only prayed for what he felt God would answer.

   • Have you ever done similar things in your prayer experience with God? Explain.

   • What has happened when you have tried to manipulate God or to hide what was really in your heart when you prayed?

3. What can happen when we approach life (and prayer) like "a problem to be solved" rather than, as Dorothy Sayers says, "a work to be made"?

Why do you think we so often approach God in a problem-solving mode?

4. What role do you think "surprising" answers to prayer may play in changing our relationship with God and our approach to life? (MEMORY JOGGER: What did Joni Eareckson Tada say about how her life changed the day she suffered a broken neck?)

Bible Exploration

Keeping Company with God When Our Prayers Go Unanswered

> The assurance of answered prayers, still sweeping in its scope, comes with conditions. Am I abiding in Christ? Am I making requests according to his will? Am I obeying his commands? Each of these underscores the relationship, the companionship with God. The more we know God, the more we know God's will, the more likely our prayers will align with that will.
>
> *Prayer*, p. 235

1. When we are hurting or are in great need, it can be difficult to consider the possibility that our actions or attitudes may actually hinder our prayers, yet that is exactly what the Bible tells us.

   • Read Psalm 66:18; Isaiah 1:15–17; 59:1–2; Zechariah 7:8–13; and James 4:3. What do you learn from these passages about the effect that disobedience has on God's willingness to hear — and respond to — our prayers?

   • How seriously, then, do we need to take the responsibility to examine our hearts and lives and deal with sin and other blockages? How does doing so nurture the relationship God desires to have with us?

2. Although God takes sin seriously, God also promises forgiveness and abundant mercy. God welcomes those who desire to restore their relationship with him.

   • Read Psalm 32:1–5; Proverbs 28:13; and 1 John 1:7, 9. How does God say we can restore a broken relationship?

   • What do these Bible passages show you about how much God values a restored relationship with us?

3. What qualifying conditions for answered prayer do you note in the following prayer promises? What do these passages reveal to you about answered prayer and keeping company with God?

Bible Passage	The Condition	The Result(s)	The Relationship
John 15:5–8			
John 15:10–16			
1 John 3:21–24			

Closing Group Discovery Discussion

Prayer remains a struggle for me. On the other hand, so does forgiving someone who has wronged me. So does loving my neighbor. So does caring for the needy. I persist because I am fulfilling God's command, and also because I believe I am doing what is best for me whether or not I feel like it at the time. Moreover, I believe that my perseverance, in some unfathomable way, brings pleasure to God. We should always pray and not give up, Jesus taught.

Prayer, p. 161

Although praying with persistence can seem like a challenge, Jesus emphasized it in several of his teachings (Matthew 13:44–46; Luke 11:5–10; 18:1–8) and by his life example (Matthew 15:21–28). Philip notes that God views "persistence as a sign of genuine desire for change, the one prerequisite for spiritual growth."

But what about us? Philip observes in his own life that "When I really want something, I strive and persist. Whether it's climbing Colorado's mountains, chasing the woodpeckers away from my roof, or getting a high-speed Internet connection for my home, I'll do whatever it takes." He then wonders, "Do I show the same spirit in prayer?"

To what extent do you value persistent prayer and sacrifice for it? How closely aligned do you think your view of persistent prayer is to God's view?

WRAP-UP (10 MINUTES)

DVD Wrap-up by Philip Yancey

Personal Reflection

> Keeping company with God includes far more than the time I devote to prayer each day. God is alive all day, living both around me and inside me, speaking in a still, small voice and in other ways I may not even recognize. God is not really silent, we are deaf, says Teresa of Avila. If so, my job is to remain vigilant like a sentry on duty, straining to hear the sounds of the night as well as the first signs of dawn.
>
> *Prayer*, pp. 202–203

Sooner or later, everyone who prays will experience difficult times when God seems hopelessly distant, when the act of prayer seems futile, or when it seems as if God is simply unwilling to answer heartfelt prayers. The psalmist David felt such a barrier when he cried, "How long, LORD? Will you forget me forever? How long will you hide your face from me? How long must I wrestle with my thoughts and day after day have sorrow in my heart?... Look on me and answer, LORD my God" (Psalm 13:1–3).

For the next few minutes, *consider the barriers* you currently are feeling in your prayer experience.

Then think about *how you have responded* to these particular difficulties.

Next, think about the approach to prayer Philip has found helpful when he faces unanswered prayer and other prayer problems—*keep it short, keep it honest, keep it going.*

Finally, *consider new ways you could respond* to these difficulties. Some might include:

- Clearing up your channels of communication with God through confession and repentance of wrongdoing
- Examining your prayer motives to see how closely they are aligned with God's
- Viewing prayer as a means of seeking companionship with God, not just as a way of getting results
- Taking steps to keep close company with God each day so that you can be more in tune with who God is and what God is doing in your life
- Choosing to trust God and be honest in your prayers despite how you may be feeling
- Asking God to use a time of spiritual dryness to prepare you for future growth
- Believing that God is listening and that God cares about what is important to you
- Looking for surprises that may come from God during this time of waiting and perseverance

Group Prayer

Begin by praying aloud Psalms 88:1–2 and 86:1–4:

> LORD, you are the God who saves me; day and night I cry out to you. May my prayer come before you; turn your ear to my cry.... Hear me, LORD, and answer me, for I am poor and needy. Guard my life, for I am faithful to you; save your servant who trusts in you. You are my God; have mercy on me, Lord, for I call to you all day long. Bring joy to your servant, Lord, for I put my trust in you.

Now continue to pray, focusing on who God is, the Bible's promises about prayer, and what you are learning through this session. If you feel comfortable doing so, pray together about some of the prayer barriers with which you struggle. Open up and express what you'd like God to do in you and for one another. Pray that God would teach you and that you would be willing students, so that those troublesome barriers can become stepping-stones to growth and avenues for keeping company with God.

PERSONAL JOURNEY: TO DO ON YOUR OWN

The only final solution to unanswered prayer is Paul's explanation to the Corinthians: "For now we see through a glass, darkly; but then face to face: now I know in part; but then shall I know even as also I am known." No human being, no matter how wise or how spiritual, can interpret the ways of God, explaining why one miracle and not another, why an apparent intervention here and not there. Along with the apostle Paul, we can only wait, and trust.

Prayer, p. 247

Bible Discovery

Even Christians advanced in the spiritual disciplines still struggle with prayer. Times when the dialogue of prayer seems stilted or its results are difficult to see can be terribly discouraging. But even then, God encourages us to pray. After all, prayer expresses relationship and relationship takes work. If we are to experience the times of ecstasy and fulfillment in prayer, we must also persevere through dark nights and periods of spiritual dryness.

1. If you are struggling with unanswered prayer, it is of course important to determine if you are harboring sin that is blocking God's response. But remember that God's response is not solely dependent on us. Even Jesus, who was sinless, prayed prayers that God didn't answer as Jesus wished. So look at the prayers and answers on page 81 to see what you learn about unanswered prayer.

The Prayer (Who Prayed? For What?)	The Result	My Understanding of What Happened
Ex. 2:23–25	Ex. 3:7–10	
2 Sam. 12:15–17	2 Sam. 12:18–24	
1 Kings 19:1–5	1 Kings 19:5–7	
Dan. 9:1–3	Dan. 10:4–6, 11–14	
Matt. 26:39	Matt. 27:32–39	
Luke 22:32	John 18:15–17, 25–27	
John 17:20–21	Rom. 16:17; 1 Cor. 1:10–11	
2 Cor. 12:7–8	2 Cor. 12:9	

2. We're not left totally in the dark to ponder the mystery of unanswered prayer; the Bible tells us what to do when answers don't come as we would like. Read each of the following passages and consider what it would mean for you to do these things.

   • Psalm 27:14

   • Psalm 37:7

   • Romans 8:18, 22–25

   • Galatians 6:9

SUPPLEMENTAL BIBLE DISCOVERY:
Are Your Prayers on Target?

In his book, Philip includes a checklist by pastor David Mains that can help us keep our prayers on track when we experience prayer difficulties. Perhaps it will help you during your prayer struggles.

1. *What do I really want?* Am I being specific, or am I just rambling about nothing in particular?

2. *Can God grant this request?* Or is it against God's nature to do so?

3. *Have I done my part?* Or am I praying to lose weight when I haven't dieted?

4. *How is my relationship with God?* Are we on speaking terms?

5. *Who will get the credit if my request is granted?* Do I have God's interests in mind?

6. *Do I really want my prayer answered?* What would I have if I actually did get that girlfriend back?

MY PRAYER JOURNAL

The very tedium, the act of waiting itself, works to nourish in us the qualities of patience, persistence, trust, gentleness, compassion — or it may do so, if we place ourselves in the stream of God's movement on earth. It may take more faith to trust God when we do not get what we ask for than when we do.

Prayer, p. 238

As session five showed, you are likely to experience great challenges to prayer. Use the following pages not only to write down your prayer requests, but also to journal about your prayer struggles. Write about what you learn, how your relationship with God changes, and what unexpected answers God sends your way. Most important, keep praying.

Listen to my prayer, O God, do not ignore my plea;
hear me and answer me.
My thoughts trouble me and I am distraught.
PSALM 55:1 – 2

Look to the LORD and his strength; seek his face always.
1 CHRONICLES 16:11

I once heard a theologian remark that in the Gospels people approached Jesus with a question 183 times whereas he replied with a direct answer only three times. Instead, he responded with a different question, a story, or some other indirection. Evidently Jesus wants us to work out answers on our own, using the principles that he taught and lived. Prayer, I find, often operates the same way. In the difficult and sometimes frustrating act of pursuing God, changes occur in me that equip me to serve God. Maybe what I sense as abandonment is actually a form of empowerment.

Prayer, pp. 205–206

DOES PRAYER CHANGE ANYTHING?

Let the morning bring me word of your unfailing love,
for I have put my trust in you.
Show me the way I should go, for to you I entrust my life....
Teach me to do your will, for you are my God;
may your good Spirit lead me on level ground.
PSALM 143:8, 10

INTRODUCTION (6 MINUTES)

DVD Introduction by Philip Yancey

Questions to Think About

- What do we normally expect when we pray and ask that God's will be done about to a specific concern?

- To what extent do we anticipate that God will accomplish what we ask through *our* labor and sacrifice?

- In what ways might our perspective on praying for God's will to be done change when we actually become partners with God in accomplishing it?

GROUP DISCOVERY (38 MINUTES)

DVD Teaching Notes

What is the "angle of repose"?

The power of accumulated prayer

Our part in a holy partnership

Finding balance in prayer and action

Making God's presence visible

DVD Discussion

As partners in God's work on earth, we insist that God's will be done while at the same time committing ourselves to whatever that may require of us. "Your kingdom come, your will be done," Jesus taught us to pray. These words are not placid invocations; they are demands expressed in the imperative mood. Give us justice! Set the world aright! God has called out partners on earth to serve as messengers of the kingdom, heralds of a world on the way to healing and redemption.

Prayer, p. 112

1. Consider for a moment the "angle of repose" idea Philip presented in relationship to prayer. (MEMORY JOGGER: In geological terms, the angle of repose is the position at which a rock is poised between resting motionless on a slope or tumbling down the mountainside.)

   • What role do you think persevering prayer can have in shifting the angle of repose to create a noticeable impact on what God seeks to accomplish here on earth?

   • When have you seen this happen?

2. When have you seen God accomplish things through people rather than miraculously "fixing" a situation, and what role did praying people play in accomplishing God's will in those instances?

3. Philip mentions a "holy partnership" between us and God in prayer. In what ways might our prayers and our lives change if we were to bring needs before God and listen to how God might want *us* to join in partnership to meet those needs?

Bible Exploration
We Are Partners in God's Work

God has indeed played a direct role in manipulating natural events: causing a drought or a plague of locusts, reversing the course of disease and disability, even restoring life to a corpse. Apart from these rare events called miracles, however, the Bible emphasizes an ongoing providence, of God's will being done through the common course of nature and ordinary human activity: rain falling and seeds sprouting, farmers planting and harvesting, the strong caring for the weak, the haves giving to the have-nots, the healthy ministering to the sick. We tend to place God's activity in a different category from natural or human activity; the Bible tends to draw them together. Somehow God works in all of creation, all of history, to bring about ultimate goals.

Prayer, p. 139

1. In Matthew 6:9 – 10, Jesus prayed about the will of his Father being done on earth. Although we may tend to think in terms of us doing the praying and God miraculously doing the work, God has a long history of accomplishing his will through people. (And God often calls on the

people who have done the praying to do the work!) Read Exodus 3:1–2, 7–10; Judges 4:1–7, 14–16; 6:1–6, 11–16; and Nehemiah 1:1–4; 2:1–6; 6:15–16 to discover how God often works.

• How did God's will get carried out in each circumstance?

• What possibilities do these examples raise in regard to your prayers and how God might want to work in partnership with you?

2. When Jesus was teaching his disciples, he left no doubt as to whom God would rely on to carry out the work of his kingdom (see Luke 10:2–3). How well do you think we Christians understand and respond to the balance of prayer and action that the Bible mandates for accomplishing God's will? Explain your answer.

3. Throughout the Bible, God clearly demonstrates concern for the poor and needy and desires us to join the stream of love and comfort to meet their needs.

   • Read the following passages and note how the early Christians went about accomplishing God's will in this regard.
   • Discuss the role Christians today have in partnership with God to care for the poor and needy. What is the proper relationship between our prayers and actions, and what might accomplishing God's will look like in our world?

Bible Passage	Early Christians' Response to the Needy	Joining with God to Accomplish His Will Today
Acts 2:45; 4:34–35		
Rom. 12:13		
James 2:15–17		
1 John 3:17–18		

4. Which metaphor is often used in the New Testament to show that God has chosen to use people who embody Christ to dispense grace and love to a needy world? (See 1 Corinthians 12:27; Ephesians 4:11–12.)

Closing Group Discovery Discussion

> To call God and me unequal partners is a laughable understatement. And yet by inviting us to do kingdom work on earth, God has indeed set up a kind of odd-couple alliance. God delegates work to human beings so that we do history together, so to speak.... [Our] relationship with God [is] based on constant negotiation. We inform God what we think should be done in the world, and in the process God reminds us of our own role in doing it.
>
> *Prayer*, pp. 66, 241

God uses a special term to describe those who have joined in partnership to accomplish kingdom work on earth. Do you know what it is? Think for a moment of Abraham and Moses. The Bible speaks of them as being *friends of God*. What an honor and privilege to be a friend of God!

As unbelievable as it may seem, *friend* is a designation that Jesus freely gives to those who follow and obey him: "You are my friends if you do what I command. I no longer call you servants, because servants do not know their master's business. Instead, I have called you friends, for everything that I learned from my Father I have made known to you" (John 15:14–15).

Jesus asks each believer to take partnership in God's work on earth. As we do so, we can picture God as our friend. We can converse with God through prayer, which Philip refers to as the "currency" of our friendship with God. Take a few minutes now to share your insights into the partnership God longs to have with each of us in accomplishing God's kingdom work on earth. You might ask:

In what ways does being a friend of God change:
- my understanding of prayer?
- what I pray for?
- how diligently I pray?
- how carefully I listen to God when I pray?
- how honestly I pray?
- how eagerly I pray?
- how much I long to keep company with God?

WRAP-UP (11 MINUTES)

DVD Wrap-up by Philip Yancey

Personal Reflection

> I see prayer as the process of becoming available for what God wants to do on earth through us.... God wants to do miracles every day through us, if we only make ourselves available.
>
> Bud, quoted in *Prayer*, pp. 266–277

If you are a Christian, you are part of Christ's body (literally God's presence on earth) — the hands and feet God has called to participate in a holy partnership to accomplish the work of God's kingdom. As Philip observes in the video, "There comes a time when meditation has to turn into action. Indeed, I've found that a lot of the questions that I present to God, God turns right back to me. 'What about poverty in the world? What about people who are suffering? What about those who have no one to love them?' And as I present those concerns to God, I hear this voice saying, 'Yes, Philip, what about them? What are *you* doing about those people?'"

Use the next few moments to read Mark 1:35–38; Acts 13:1–5; and Romans 1:8–12, which give a taste of the relationship between our prayers and taking action to carry out God's will.

Now consider the prayers you have prayed and are praying. Pray about the action(s) God may want you to take:

- Your willingness to join in what God desires to accomplish through you
- Ways in which you can make God, who is already present, more visible to others around you
- Your commitment to keep close company with God
- Your desire to seek a better understanding of and commitment to the work God wants to do on this earth

Group Prayer

Begin by praying aloud Psalm 112:1, 4–6:

> Praise the LORD.... Even in darkness light dawns for the upright, for those who are gracious and compassionate and righteous. Good will come to those who are generous and lend freely, who conduct their affairs with justice. Surely the righteous will never be shaken; they will be remembered forever.

Now continue to pray, focusing on what God has been saying to you during this session. Add your voice to the stream of God's work on earth. Pray for what you know God desires—the specific people, needs, and circumstances that are close to God's heart. Pray that the desires of your heart will be aligned with the desires of God's heart. Pray about how you can become a "divine partner" to accomplish God's will on earth.

PERSONAL JOURNEY: TO DO ON YOUR OWN

Prayer may seem at first like disengagement, a reflective time to consider God's point of view. But that vantage presses us back to accomplish God's will, the work of the kingdom. We are God's fellow workers, and as such we turn to prayer to equip us for the partnership.... [Just as] Jesus counted on prayer as a source of strength that equipped him to carry out a partnership with God the Father on earth, [we, too, depend on that relationship.]

Prayer, pp. 128, 58

Bible Discovery

Throughout the six sessions of this study, you have explored various aspects of prayer, the character of God, and yourself. Yet what you have learned is just a beginning, a preparation for a lifetime of opportunities to keep company with the God of the universe. Right now prayer may be an awkward rehearsal for what is to come. The connection between you and God may be a bit garbled and intermittent.

But prayer is God's designated way of closing the gap. Prayer brings us into God's presence, giving us a glimpse of life from a divine vantage point. Prayer changes us and our experience of life. Prayer launches us into the stream of kingdom work and helps us make God visible on earth.

1. Making God visible on earth is a high calling. Read the stories of the following people whom God called to help make his presence "visible" to others around them. Allow these stories to encourage you as you pray and seek to make God visible in your everyday world.

   • Moses (Exodus 12:31 – 32; 14:23 – 28; 18:1, 7 – 12)

- Elijah (1 Kings 17:17–24)

- Daniel (Daniel 6:13–28)

- The early Christians (Acts 2:42–47)

2. Participating in the holy partnership involves offering up our prayer requests and trusting God to incorporate them into a plan of action that accomplishes God's will. But as many martyrs have learned, prayer is a means of getting God's will done on earth, not ours. As you pray for God's will to be done, meditate on the following passages that reveal what our attitude should be toward whatever action God chooses.

- Luke 22:42

- Daniel 3:16–18

SUPPLEMENTAL BIBLE DISCOVERY:
The Promise of Partnership

Prayer is cooperation with God, a consent that opens the way for grace to work. Although such a partnership with God may lack the drama of God's bargaining sessions with Abraham and Moses, notice what the apostle Paul shares about the close-knit communion that results from our partnership with God.

- 1 Corinthians 15:10

- Galatians 2:20

- Ephesians 2:10

- Philippians 2:12 – 13

MY PRAYER JOURNAL

In prayer [I] stand before God to plead [my] condition as well as the conditions around [me]. In the process, the act of prayer emboldens me to join the work of transforming the world into a place where the Father's will is indeed done as it is in heaven. We are Christ's body on earth, after all; he has no hands but ours. And yet to act as Christ's body we need an unbroken connection to the Head. We pray in order to see the world with God's eyes, and then to join the stream of power as it breaks loose.

Prayer, p. 124

God always longs to hear from you! One day each of us will have the chance to talk face to face with God, the Creator who loves us, is redeeming us, and truly desires an ongoing relationship with us. In the meantime, we have the privilege of "showing up" in prayer to commune with God. We have confidence that God listens to us and indeed longs to engage us in a holy partnership to do on earth what is done in heaven.

Use these pages to write down prayer requests, things you are discovering about keeping company with God, how prayer is changing you, and what role God may have for you in doing kingdom work on this needy planet.

_____

_____

_____

_____

_____

_____

_____

_____

_____

_____

I desire to do your will, my God; your law is within my heart.
PSALM 40:8

I waited patiently for the LORD; he turned to me and heard my cry....
He put a new song in my mouth, a hymn of praise to our God.
Many will see and fear the LORD and put their trust in him.

PSALM 40:1, 3

My perspective has changed as I understand prayer as partnership, a subtle interplay of human and divine that accomplishes God's work on earth. God asks me to make myself known to him in prayer and then works my prayers into a master plan for my life — a plan which I can only faintly grasp.

Prayer, p. 113

PRAYER RESOURCES

Compiled by Philip Yancey

There are thousands of resources on prayer, ranging from Richard Wagner's *Christian Prayer for Dummies* to Friedrich Heiler's exhaustive *Prayer* and the recent bestseller *Prayer: A History* by Philip and Carol Zaleski. I can only mention a sampling, most of which can be located by an Internet search.

Prayer, by Richard Foster, examines twenty-one different kinds of prayer. Foster's organization, Renovaré, publishes *Spiritual Classics* and *Devotional Classics,* which contain time-tested writings on the spiritual disciplines.

Peter Kreeft's *Prayer for Beginners* answers basic questions, as does Marjorie J. Thompson's *Soul Feast.* Donald Bloesch's *The Struggle of Prayer* and P. T. Forsyth's *The Soul of Prayer* investigate obstacles the serious pray-er may encounter. Simon Tugwell and Thomas H. Green have written several encouraging books for those who struggle with frustration and dryness in prayer. *The Art of Prayer* by Timothy Jones takes a more personal and pastoral approach. *Prayer and Temperament* by Chester Michael and Marie Norrisey, mentioned in chapter 14 of *Prayer: Does It Make Any Difference?,* gives guidance to different personalities, following the Myers-Briggs Type Indicator test (MBTI). Others I recommend: *Contemplative Prayer* by Thomas Merton; *Dimensions of Prayer* by Douglas Van Steere; *The Problem with Prayer Is,* by David Hubbard; *The Still Hour,* by Austin Phelps; *Prayer, the Divine Dialog,* by Carroll Simcox; *The God Who Speaks,* by Ben Campbell Johnson; *With Christ in the School of Prayer,* by Andrew Murray.

Hans Urs von Balthasar and Karl Rahner have contributed insightful (though dense) books from a Catholic perspective. Orthodox theologian Anthony Bloom penned several rewarding books on prayer. E. M. Bounds wrote eight (rather repetitive) books on prayer in the nineteenth century, now published in one volume. George A. Buttrick's *Prayer* is no longer in print, but will prove worth the hunt if you can find a used edition. Esther de Waal sheds light on a rich tradition in *The Celtic Way of Prayer.*

A website based in the U.K., *www.24-7prayer.com*, offers a global perspective on prayer. Indeed, any Internet search engine can lead you to a host of websites specializing in prayer.

The Upper Room, based in Nashville, Tennessee, publishes numerous resources on spiritual disciplines, most notably the journal *Weavings* and excellent workbooks on prayer by Maxie Dunnam. *Armchair Mystic* by the Jesuit priest Mark E. Thibodeaux gives a short and immensely practical guide to meditative prayer. Alice Fryling's *The Art of Spiritual Listening* approaches the same subject from an evangelical perspective.

For those more philosophically inclined, *Providence and Prayer* by Terrance Tiessen explores every angle of the Calvinist/Arminian/Open Theology debates on prayer. And C. S. Lewis's *Letters to Malcolm: Chiefly on Prayer* brilliantly tackles both practical and theoretical issues. I also recommend *Creative Prayer*, by Brigid E. Herman; *Doors into Prayer*, by Emilie Griffin; *Gratefulness, the Heart of Prayer*, by Brother David Steindl-Rast; and *When God Doesn't Answer Your Prayer*, by Jerry Sittser.

In *Bless This House*, Gregory and Suzanne M. Wolfe assemble a delightful collection of prayers for families to use in teaching children the art of prayer. Betty Shannon Cloyd's *Children and Prayer: A Shared Pilgrimage* also addresses this need.

COLLECTIONS

Some collections focus on individuals: *The Prayers of Kierkegaard*, edited by Perry D. LeFevre; *Lancelot Andrews and His Private Devotions*, translated by Alexander Whyte; *The English Poems of George Herbert*, edited by C. A. Patrides; *Prayers from The Imitation of Christ* by Thomas à Kempis, edited by Ronald Klug; and John Donne's *Devotions*. The website *www.wordamongus .org* has information on the "Praying with" series that features prayers by such notables as C. S. Lewis, Ignatius of Loyola, and Dorothy Day.

Catholics produce *Christian Prayer: Liturgy of the Hours* while Anglicans and Episcopalians rely on the *Book of Common Prayer*, both excellent resources designed for liturgical use. *A Guide to Prayer for All Who Seek God* follows a similar format, drawing on both contemporary and classic writings; and many denominations publish their own prayer guides. See also the *Book of Common Worship*, by Westminster John Knox Press; *A Treasury of Prayers*, by Stephen Fortosis; and *The Oxford Book of Prayer*, edited by George Appleton.

Phyllis Tickle has streamlined the Divine Hours liturgy in a popular trilogy of books. Kathleen Norris's *The Cloister Walk* and Robert Benson's *Living Prayer* give the story behind two people who encounter the liturgy; Benson later did his own collection in *Venite: A Book of Daily Prayer.*

The Lion Prayer Collection compiled by Mary Batchelor groups over 1,300 prayers according to topic. Ken Gire's *Between Heaven and Earth* includes many sample prayers as well as brief reflections on the subject. John Baillie's *A Diary of Private Prayer* offers contemporary prayers, one for morning and evening, with blank pages for the reader's own notes. Benedict Groeschel's *Praying to Our Lord Jesus Christ* brings together written prayers and meditations from the second to the twentieth century, most by Catholic luminaries.

BIBLE MEDITATION

Thelma Hall's *Too Deep for Words: Rediscovering Lectio Divina* includes five hundred Scripture texts that can be prayed in a contemplative way. Eugene Peterson's *Eat This Book* includes several chapters on the *lectio divina* style of meditating on Bible passages, while Richard Peace's *Contemplative Bible Reading* tailors the method to small group study.

Eugene Peterson has also written several books on the Psalms, including one that gives a year of daily prayers and reflections. *Christ in the Psalms,* by the Orthodox priest Patrick Henry Reardon, goes through the psalms one by one.

What's So Amazing About Grace?

A 10-Session Investigation of Grace

Philip Yancey

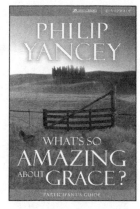

In this curriculum based on *What's So Amazing About Grace?* award-winning author Philip Yancey explores grace at street level. If grace is God's love for the undeserving, he asks, then what does it look like in action? And if Christians are its sole dispensers, then how are we doing at lavishing grace on a world that knows far more of cruelty and unforgiveness than it does of mercy?

Small Group Edition DVD with Leader's Guide   0-310-26179-1
Participant's Guide   0-310-23325-9

The Bible Jesus Read

An 8-Session Exploration of the Old Testament

Philip Yancey

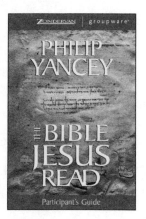

This DVD curriculum explores the sometimes shocking and cryptic writings of the Old Testament to help readers know God better. Yancey serves as guide and interpretive leader of each session and, in a series of in-depth interviews and explanations, he covers five crucial segments of the Old Testament:

- Job: Seeing in the Dark
- Deuteronomy: A Taste of Bittersweet
- Psalms: Spirituality in Every Key
- Ecclesiastes: The End of Wisdom
- The Prophets: God Talks Back

Small Group Edition DVD with Leader's Guide   0-310-27521-0
Participant's Guide   0-310-24185-5

When God's People Pray

6 Sessions on the Transforming Power of Prayer

Jim Cymbala, Bestselling Author of Fresh Wind, Fresh Fire

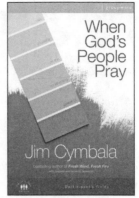

Prayer can change lives and circumstances like nothing else can. What are the keys that unlock its power, that turn prayer from a mere activity into a vital link with God and all his resources? In this DVD, Jim Cymbala, pastor of the Brooklyn Tabernacle, shows you and your small group truths about prayer that God has used to turn his own church from a tiny, struggling inner-city congregation into a vital, thriving community of believers who pray with passion, focus, and faith.

DVD-ROM with Leader's Guide 0-310-26735-8
Participant's Guide 0-310-26734-X

Zondervan Legacy Series
John Stott on the Bible and the Christian Life

Six Sessions on the Authority, Interpretation, and Use of Scripture

John Stott

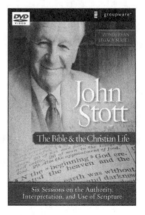

In this six-session DVD curriculum, author and pastor John R. W. Stott—recently named one of the 100 most influential people in the world by *Time* magazine—addresses key areas of Christian beliefs in his typical clear, balanced, biblically based, and intellectually rigorous manner. Includes discussion guide.

DVD 0-310-27297-1

Faith Lessons Vols. 6 and 7

In the Dust of the Rabbi, Walk as Jesus Walked

Ray Vander Laan

Filmed on location in Israel and Turkey, the two newest additions to this well-loved DVD series take your small group to the times and customs of the ancient world in which the first-century followers of Jesus lived. Each DVD features 5 sessions led by teacher Ray VanderLaan. The corresponding Discovery Guide for each volume includes sidebars, maps, photos, and other study tools to help you understand the meaning of the biblical text better, plus 25 personal Bible studies designed to help you deepen your learning experience between sessions.

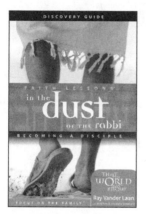

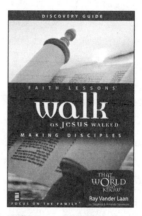

In the Dust of the Rabbi
DVD with Leader's Guide 0-310-27119-3
Discovery Guide 0-310-27120-7

Walk as Jesus Walked
DVD with Leader's Guide 0-310-27116-9
Discovery Guide 0-310-27117-7

Pick up a copy today at your favorite bookstore!

ZONDERVAN®
.com

Deeper Connections
The Miracles of Jesus, The Parables of Jesus, The Prayers of Jesus
In-Depth Studies Connecting the Bible to Life
Matt Williams, General Editor

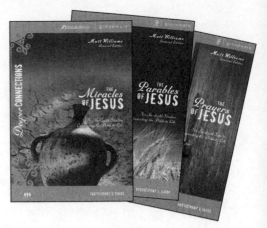

The Deeper Connections series is unique. Unlike any other Bible study available, this visually stunning DVD series is written and taught by biblical experts—six professors with specialized areas of knowledge. Hosted by Jarrett Stevens, who introduces each session from Israel, and filmed in locations as diverse as the Rocky Mountains, Gloucester Harbor, the California coast, Boston's Old North Church, and Chicago's lakefront, each volume consists of six fascinating sessions. Each session is taught by a different instructor and consists of three components:

1. Historical background and culture
2. An engaging, close look at the biblical text and its meaning
3. Accurate, encouraging, and challenging applications of the Bible's message to life today

The participant's guide for each book includes maps and pictures, outlines, key Scripture verses, discussion questions, plenty of room for note taking, and a personal five-day Bible study for each session.

The teachers:

Dr. Gary Burge, Wheaton College
Dr. David Garland, Truett Theological Seminary
Dr. Mark Strauss, Bethel Seminary
Dr. Michael Wilkins, Talbot School of Theology
Dr. Matt Williams, Biola University
Dr. Ben Witherington III, Asbury Theological Seminary

The Miracles of Jesus
DVD with Leader's Guide 0-310-27193-2
Participant's Guide 0-310-27194-0

The Parables of Jesus
DVD with Leader's Guide 0-310-27190-8
Participant's Guide 0-310-27191-6

The Prayers of Jesus
DVD with Leader's Guide 0-310-27196-7
Participant's Guide 0-310-27197-5

We want to hear from you. Please send your comments about this book to us in care of zreview@zondervan.com. Thank you.

ZONDERVAN.com/
AUTHORTRACKER
follow your favorite authors